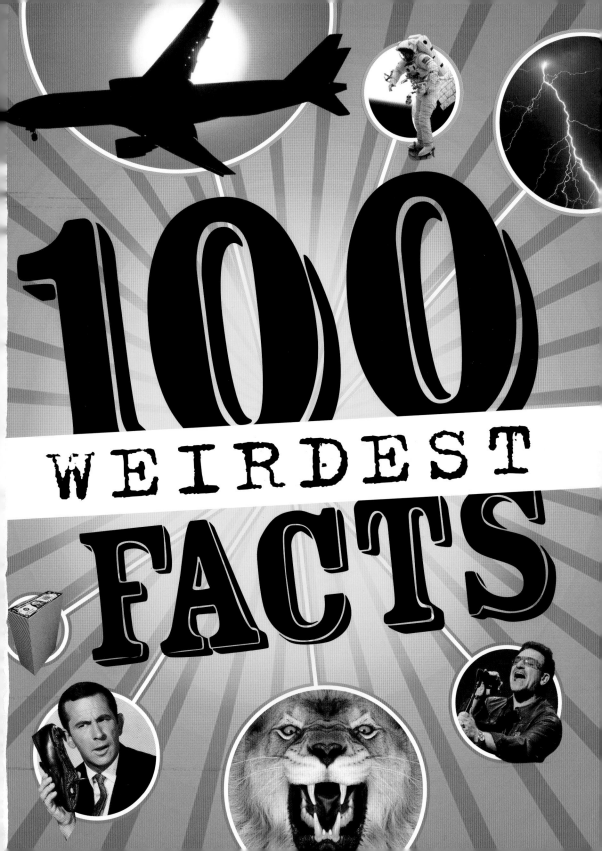

100

WEIRDEST

FACTS

Editorial and Design: Dynamo Ltd and Fineline
QEB Project Editor: Alexandra Koken

First published in the United States in 2013 by
QEB Publishing, Inc.
3 Wrigley, Suite A,
Irvine, CA 92618

www.qed-publishing.co.uk

A CIP record for this book is available from the Library of Congress.

ISBN 978 1 60992 464 5

Printed in China

100 WEIRDEST FACTS

QEB

QEB Publishing

CONTENTS

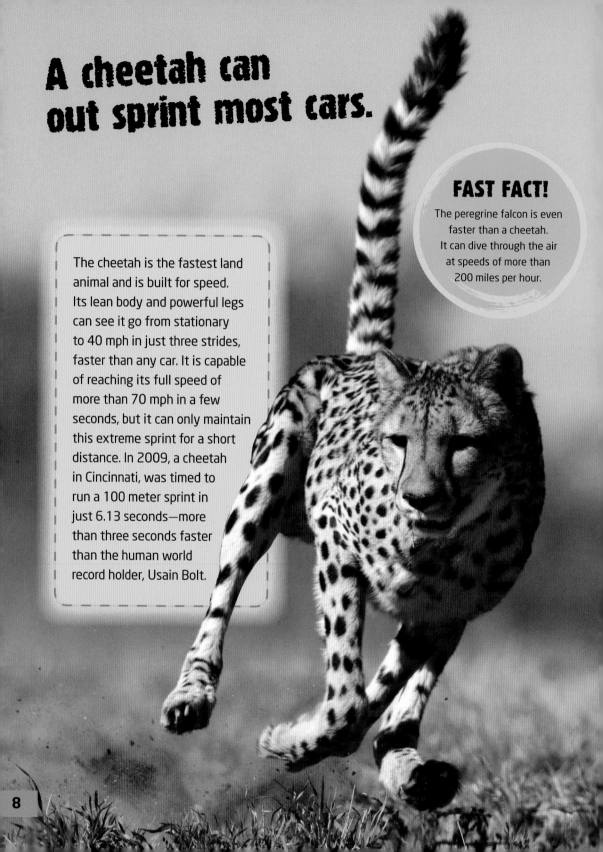

A cheetah can out sprint most cars.

The cheetah is the fastest land animal and is built for speed. Its lean body and powerful legs can see it go from stationary to 40 mph in just three strides, faster than any car. It is capable of reaching its full speed of more than 70 mph in a few seconds, but it can only maintain this extreme sprint for a short distance. In 2009, a cheetah in Cincinnati, was timed to run a 100 meter sprint in just 6.13 seconds—more than three seconds faster than the human world record holder, Usain Bolt.

FAST FACT!

The peregrine falcon is even faster than a cheetah. It can dive through the air at speeds of more than 200 miles per hour.

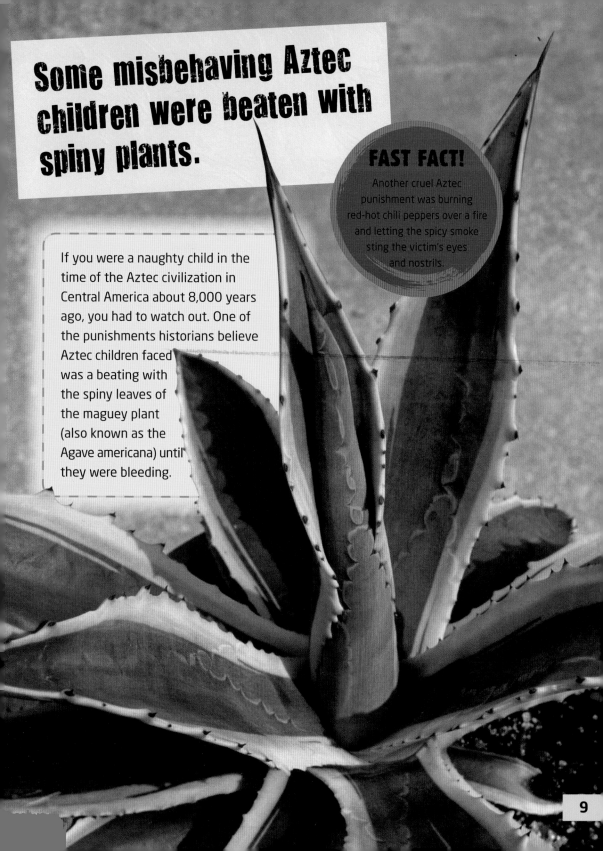

Some misbehaving Aztec children were beaten with spiny plants.

If you were a naughty child in the time of the Aztec civilization in Central America about 8,000 years ago, you had to watch out. One of the punishments historians believe Aztec children faced was a beating with the spiny leaves of the maguey plant (also known as the Agave americana) until they were bleeding.

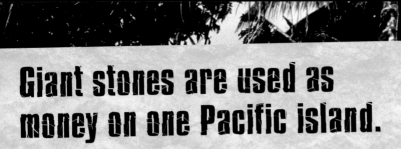

Giant stones are used as money on one Pacific island.

The small Pacific island of Yap, one of the Caroline Islands, has an unusual currency. Stone discs, carved out of calcite rock, were commonly used to buy goods and services in the past, although today the U.S. dollar is mostly used.

What makes Yap's stone money really interesting is how H-U-G-E some of the stones are. The largest measures 12 feet in diameter and needs more than a dozen adults to lift it.

FAST FACT!

The first paper money was used about 1,200 years ago in China during the Tang Dynasty.

FAST FACT!

The origin of the word *flag* comes from the Saxon word *fflake*—meaning to fly or float in the air.

National flags come in all colors and designs. The only square flags are those of Switzerland and the Vatican City, while Mozambique's is the only national flag to feature a firearm, an AK-47 rifle, on its design.

Vatican City flag

Mozambique flag

The flag of the South Asian nation of Nepal was officially introduced in 1962. It has five sides and looks like two triangles stacked on top of each other.

You cannot tickle yourself.

Most people are ticklish and have a special spot—perhaps their belly, their armpits, or the backs of their knees —that makes them giggle when it's tickled by someone else. But no matter how hard you try, you cannot tickle yourself.

Scientists think that the answer lies in a part of the brain called the cerebellum. This area performs lots of different tasks, such as controlling your balance and movement. It may also help you to ignore and not react to sensations you expect—like when you attempt to tickle yourself.

More than 3 million emails are sent around the world every single second.

It is believed that the first email was sent by a U.S. computer programmer called Ray Tomlinson in 1971. At the time, it wasn't thought of as a big deal, but as more and more people got computers and had access to the Internet, emails became the perfect way to send messages, photographs, or other computer files to people all around the world.

More than 2 billion people have one or more email accounts, and about 280 billion emails are sent every day– more than 3 million per second.

Leonardo da Vinci wrote his notes backward.

A gifted artist, inventor, and thinker, Leonardo da Vinci filled his notebooks with backward writing, which could only be read using a mirror. There are more than 6,000 pages of these notes in existence. Among da Vinci's amazing achievements were designs for flying machines and tanks, amazing anatomical drawings of the human body, and famous paintings such as the *Mona Lisa*.

FAST FACT!

The *Mona Lisa* has been stolen and vandalized on a number of occasions, and it once even went missing for two years. Now it sits safely at the Louvre Museum in Paris, France.

An ice hockey puck struck by Zdeno Chára of the Boston Bruins reached a speed of 108.8 mph.

FAST FACT!

Some early hockey pucks were made of wood. The first rubber puck was used in a match held in Montreal, Canada, in 1875.

At 6 foot 9 inches tall, the Slovakian defender Zdeno Chára is the tallest player to compete in the National Hockey League (NHL).

In 2009, Chára hit the hardest ever shot of 105.4 mph during the Superskills Competition in Montreal, Canada. Three years later, in Ottawa, he broke his own record with a shot of 108.8 mph, which is the hardest recorded NHL shot today.

Walt Disney banned his staff from growing mustaches for 40 years.

Walt Disney had a mustache himself, but he wanted the staff at his theme parks to convey a clean-cut image. So, in the mid-1950s he introduced a staff dress code that banned beards, long hair, and mustaches. Even though Disney died in 1966, the ban on mustaches remained in place and wasn't lifted until 2000. The ban on beards was only removed in 2012.

FAST FACT!

Walt Disney has had more nominations for Oscars than any other person— a staggering 59 in total.

A man was struck by lightning SEVEN different times and survived them all.

Roy Sullivan was 30 years old when he was first struck by lightning in 1942. By 1977, the U.S. park ranger, who worked at Shenandoah National Park in Virginia, had suffered an incredible seven lightning strikes. Some occurred while working in the park, but the last happened while he was out fishing. Most left parts of his body scorched, although the fourth strike in 1972 set his hair on fire. Sullivan's wife was also struck once by lightning, while she was hanging out the laundry.

FAST FACT!

Lightning is a sudden discharge of electricity. This can heat up the air to very high temperatures—more than than 40,000 °F.

A man tied 45 helium balloons to a lawn chair and ended up flying more than 2.8 miles into the air.

In 1982, Larry Walters decided to take off from his yard in San Pedro, California. He attached his lawn chair to a bunch of 8-foot-wide balloons filled with helium—a gas that's lighter than air—and rose to an altitude of nearly 3 miles. He shot some of the balloons with a pellet gun to descend, but accidentally dropped the gun. Eventually, his balloons got tangled up in a power line, causing a 20-minute electricity blackout. Amazingly, he made it safely back down to the ground.

FAST FACT!

Larry Walters always wanted to become a pilot with the United States Air Force, but couldn't because of his poor eyesight.

The shortest ever war lasted less than 45 minutes!

In 1896, British forces went to war against the forces of the Sultan of Zanzibar, an island in the Indian Ocean (now part of Tanzania). Five British ships and land forces were given the order to attack the Sultan's Palace in Zanzibar Town at nine o'clock in the morning, and firing began two minutes later. Before the clocks had reached 9:45 a.m., the war was over. The Sultan fled, and the British installed a new ruler.

FAST FACT!

The Netherlands and the Isles of Scilly, off the southwestern coast of England, were technically at war for more than 300 years, but no shots were fired.

A single ounce of gold could be stretched into a wire 50 miles long.

FAST FACT!

The Royal Canadian Mint produced the largest ever gold coin in 2007. The giant Maple Leaf coin was more than 1 inch thick and 20 inches in diameter.

Some materials are ductile, which means they can be easily drawn, or pulled, into thin wires. Gold is so ductile that just a single ounce of it could be pulled into a very thin wire 50 miles long.

Gold can also be easily worked and flattened into thin sheets. Just 1 ounce of this precious metal could be flattened into a sheet with an area more than four times the size of a ping pong table!

Blame It on the Boogie, a hit song for The Jacksons featuring Michael Jackson, was written by a different Michael Jackson.

Michael "Mick" George Jackson was a British singer-songwriter who cowrote *Blame It on the Boogie* with his brother David and Elmar Krohn. He released the song as a single in 1978–the same year in which The Jacksons released their own version of the song.

FAST FACT!

Mick Jackson was originally hoping to sell the song to Stevie Wonder.

In the 1960s, the United States and its allies were locked in secret spying battles with the Soviet Union and its supporters. The Czech secret service was on the side of the Soviets. Sometimes they would secretly intercept shoes ordered by American diplomats working in Czechoslovakia, fit a small bug inside the heel and deliver the shoes. The bugs would relay conversations to Czech spies nearby, using special listening equipment.

Diplomats' shoes were bugged by spies in the 1960s.

FAST FACT!

During the 1960s and 1970s, bugs were hidden in trees, in electrical sockets, and behind mirrors. One radio transmitter was shaped like dog poop!

The biggest known win in an adult soccer game was 149–0.

The game was played in the Madagascan League between Stade Olympique l'Emyrne, known as SOE, and newly-crowned league champions AS Adema. SOE were upset at a refereeing decision in a previous match against AS Adema, and as a protest, started scoring own goals.

FAST FACT!

The biggest win in an international football game was Australia's 2001 win against American Samoa. The score was 31-0.

In soccer, if your team lets in a goal, you get the ball back to restart play with a kick-off. AS Adema's players never got a kick as their opponents kept scoring–149 own goals in the 90-minute match. After the game, SOE's coach was suspended for three years.

More than 10 billion Android apps have been downloaded.

Android is an operating system— a set of programs that control how a digital device such as a personal computer or cell phone works.

Android was first released in 2008. It became popular because you could download small computer programs called apps (short for applications) to perform dozens of different tasks, from getting a weather forecast to playing games or music. Many of the apps available are free, and by 2011 more than 10 billion had been downloaded.

Before he became U.S. president, Andrew Jackson shot and killed a man in a duel.

In 1806, a lawyer called Charles Dickinson took part in a duel with Andrew Jackson (who became the seventh president of the United States in 1828). The pair had quarreled in Tennessee, but that state had outlawed dueling, so they crossed the state line to fight in Kentucky.

JACKSON

Jackson's single shot struck Dickinson in the chest and killed him. Dickinson's shot hit Jackson in the chest as well, but he survived. The bullet lodged close to his heart and remained inside his body for the rest of his life.

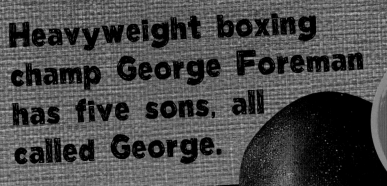

Heavyweight boxing champ George Foreman has five sons, all called George.

FAST FACT!

George Foreman won his first 40 professional fights before losing to Muhammad Ali in Kinshasa, Zaire.

American George Foreman is a boxing legend. He won an Olympic gold medal as a heavyweight as far back as 1968, and five years later knocked out Joe Frazier to become heavyweight champion of the world. In 1994, at the age of 45, he became the oldest heavyweight champion again when he defeated Michael Moorer. As well as naming his five sons George, Foreman also named one of his daughters Georgetta!

Every three seconds a ladies' purse is sold on eBay.

eBay began life as a simple auction website created by Pierre Omidyar back in 1995. The first item sold on eBay was Omidyar's old laser pen, which went for about $15 despite being broken.

FAST FACT!

eBay is used to buy and sell all sorts of things. Some weird items listed in the past include a lunch with business magnate Warren Buffet, a jet plane, and puppies!

eBay is now ENORMOUS. In 2011, $2,100-worth of goods were sold on the U.S. version of eBay every second. Globally, a purse is sold on eBay every 3 seconds, a laptop computer every 2 minutes, and a cell phone every 21 seconds.

Mercury is the closest planet to the Sun, yet temperatures can drop to as low as -279°F.

Mercury is the smallest planet in the Solar System—at 3,300 miles in diameter. Its 88-day orbit takes it as close as 29 million miles from the Sun. If you could stand on Mercury's surface, the Sun would look two-and-a-half times bigger in the sky than it does on Earth. When the Sun sets on Mercury, the temperature plummets because the planet lacks any atmosphere to trap heat.

FAST FACT!

Mercury's gravity is much lower than Earth's. If you weighed 100 pounds on Earth, then you would weigh about 37.5 pounds on Mercury.

The first microchip in 1971 held 2,300 transistors. A recent chip holds 2.6 billion!

Transistors are a crucial component used in computers and other electronic devices. In 1971, engineers managed to shrink transistors onto a single wafer of silicon to produce the first microprocessor—a device that can act as the central processing unit (CPU) of a computer.

Transistor shrinking has continued at a rapid rate, creating much faster and more powerful chips and personal computers as a result.

The first ever aircraft flight covered a distance of less than half the length of some modern passenger planes.

FAST FACT!

The entire Wright Flyer aircraft weighed just 605 pounds. Its engine generated just 12 horsepower—less than a sixth of a family car's engine today.

In 1903, at Kill Devil Hills in North Carolina, Orville Wright made the first successful aircraft flight, with his brother Wilbur watching from the ground. The 12-second flight saw the Wright Flyer travel just 120 feet— a third of the length of a football field and less than half the length of a Boeing 747-8I.

The world's biggest beaver dam is 2,790 feet long and can be viewed from space by satellites.

FAST FACT!

Beaver teeth grow continuously to counter their constant chomping on wood.

Built by generations of beavers, the world's largest beaver dam was found in 2007 using satellite images taken from space. The dam, which is in an isolated part of Wood Buffalo National Park in Northern Alberta, Canada, may have taken 40 years to construct to its current size. It is longer than eight football fields and twice as long as the Hoover Dam.

A 13-year-old boy wrote the first commercial website about soccer.

English schoolboy Tom Hadfield first used the Internet back in 1994, long before there were many sites on the World Wide Web. He realized that lots of people all over the world wanted to know the results of major soccer games, so he created the Soccernet website the following year.

In 1999, when Tom was only 17, Soccernet was sold to ESPN for a cool $40 million. Not too bad for a teen, eh?

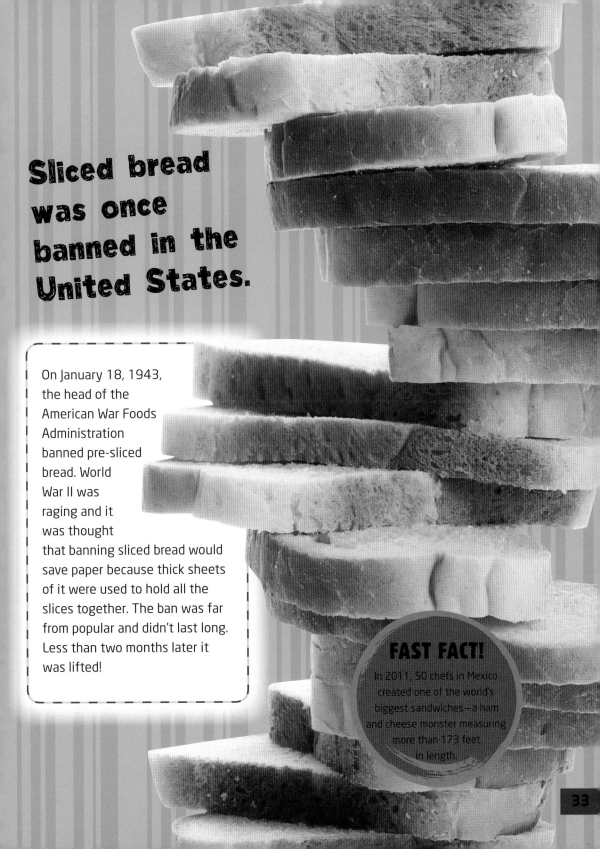

Sliced bread was once banned in the United States.

On January 18, 1943, the head of the American War Foods Administration banned pre-sliced bread. World War II was raging and it was thought that banning sliced bread would save paper because thick sheets of it were used to hold all the slices together. The ban was far from popular and didn't last long. Less than two months later it was lifted!

FAST FACT!

In 2011, 50 chefs in Mexico created one of the world's biggest sandwiches—a ham and cheese monster measuring more than 173 feet in length.

The largest meteorite ever found weighed 120,000 pounds.

Meteorites are fragments of rock from outer space that survive traveling through Earth's atmosphere and reach our planet's surface. Most are pretty small, but the specimen found in 1920 at Hoba West in the African country of Namibia was a whopper. Scientists believe it fell more than 80,000 years ago.

FAST FACT!

Many scientists believe that more than a dozen meteorites found in Antarctica originally came from Mars.

Meteorites fall every year on Earth, and in 2009, German teenager Gerrit Blank was hit on the hand by a small meteorite while walking home. He survived to tell the tale.

World War II finished in 1945, but one Japanese soldier didn't surrender until 1974.

Hiroo Onoda, shown here, was sent to Lubang Island in the Philippines with orders to carry out hit and run attacks on U.S. forces and never to surrender. True to his word, Onoda avoided capture, hid in the remote jungle and carried out occasional attacks until 1974, when his former commander, Major Taniguchi, flew to Lubang, met with Onoda and persuaded him to surrender.

FAST FACT!

After a brief stay in Japan, Onodo moved to Brazil, where he became a cattle farmer.

The blue whale's heart is as big as a small car.

Blue whales are huge! The biggest can grow to more than 100 feet in length and weigh over 400,000 pounds. Their hearts are the size of a Volkswagen Beetle car, and can weigh up to 1,300 pounds. The heart pumps blood through the arteries, some of which are more than 8 inches wide. Want one more blue whale wonder fact? Its heartbeat can be heard up to a mile away.

FAST FACT!

A blue whale's heart beats only five or six times a minute, but it pumps more than 10 tons of blood through the whale's body.

Ice speedway riders race on motorcycles without brakes, and with tires covered in spikes.

FAST FACT!

There are usually 180 to 200 spikes on the rear wheel of an ice speedway motorcycle.

Ice speedway is an exciting form of motorcycle racing around a short oval track covered in ice, usually less than 500 yards in length.

The bike tires are covered in sharp steel spikes, each up to 1.2 inches long. These spikes grip the ice and propel the bike forward. Riders reach top speeds of 80 to 90 mph on the straight sections, then angle and slide their bikes around the slippery bends. Awesome!

Computer chess programs have beaten two human world chess champions.

In 2006, Vladimir Kramnik was the undisputed chess champion of the world. He took on the Deep Fritz chess computer program and lost. The first world champion to lose to a computer was Garry Kasparov in 1997. He lost to IBM's Deep Blue computer. Deep Blue could check out 200 million chess positions per second.

FAST FACT!

Invented in 1770, the Turk—a machine that played chess—caused a sensation, but it turned out that a human was hidden inside.

Astronauts grow taller in space.

FAST FACT!
Astronauts' footprints will stay on the surface of the Moon for millions of years because there is no wind to blow them away.

An astronaut's body goes through many stresses and strains in space, especially when staying on a space station for months at a time. Gravity in space is far less than it is on Earth, which means that the forces pressing down on the spine are greatly reduced, allowing the vertebrae in your spine to spread apart a little.

Space station astronauts can grow as much as 2 inches taller, but after some time back on Earth they go back to their usual height.

Futility, a story about a giant ship called *Titan* that sinks in the Atlantic after striking an iceberg, was published **14** years before the real-life sinking of the *Titanic*.

FAST FACT!

When the *Titanic* sank, 1,517 of the 2,300 people believed to be on board died. That is almost two-thirds of the crew and passengers!

American author Morgan Robertson published his story *Futility* in 1898 and it has many spooky coincidences with the real *Titanic* disaster of 1912. Just like the *Titanic*, *Titan* was the biggest ship of its age and sank in the month of April. Both ships were powered by three propellers, had two masts, and could carry a maximum of 3,000 passengers. The *Titan* struck an iceberg at around midnight, while the *Titanic* struck an iceberg at 20 minutes to midnight.

U2 singer Bono spent $1,500 to fly his favorite hat to him in time to go on stage.

Bono was on the way to a special charity concert in Modena, Italy, hosted by opera singer Luciano Pavarotti in 2003 when he realized he didn't have his favorite hat, a trilby, with him. The singer paid for a taxi to drive the hat to London's Gatwick Airport and then paid for a first-class seat on a flight from Gatwick to Bologna in Italy. Finally, he had to spend about $200 for a taxi to drive the hat from Bologna to Modena.

FAST FACT!

Another valuable hat is the one worn in the film *Indiana Jones and the Kingdom of the Crystal Skull*, which sold at a charity auction for $19,500.

The entire country of Monaco is smaller than New York's Central Park.

The principality of Monaco is surrounded by France and the Mediterranean Sea. It is only 1,140 feet (380 yards) wide in places and has a total area of 0.76 square miles. Central Park in New York City has an area of about 1.31 square miles.

FAST FACT!

It takes less than an hour for an average person to walk across the entire country of Monaco.

The first successful expedition through the Grand Canyon was led by a one-armed war veteran.

Major John Wesley Powell was an avid explorer before taking part in the American Civil War where he lost most of his right arm at the Battle of Shiloh (1862).

Seven years later, Powell led a small party on an expedition. They traveled for more than 1,000 miles down the Green and Colorado Rivers to explore the enormous and, at the time, largely unexplored Grand Canyon.

FAST FACT!

It wasn't until Powell's second expedition in 1871 that the Grand Canyon was mapped.

Goodnight Moon author Margaret Wise Brown left her fortune to a nine-year-old neighbor.

Author Margaret Wise Brown wrote her first children's book, *When the Wind Blew*, in 1937. She wrote many children's bestsellers, such as *Goodnight Moon* and *The Runaway Bunny*, before dying at the age of 42. She left behind over 70 unpublished stories. In her will, she asked for the royalties from all her books, which over the years would total several million dollars, to go to Albert Clarke, the nine-year-old son of her neighbor in Maine.

GOODNIGHT MOON

by Margaret Wise Brown
Pictures by Clement Hurd

FAST FACT!

Goodnight Moon was one of former president George W. Bush's favorite childhood stories.

A shipwrecked man survived alone on a raft at sea for an incredible 133 days.

Poon Lim was a Chinese steward onboard the *Ben Lomond*, a merchant (non-military) ship during World War II, when a submarine torpedo sank the vessel. Poon spent a staggering four months on a small wooden life raft floating in the Atlantic Ocean.

Poon Lim survived by catching the occasional fish, and by using the canvas covering of his lifejacket to harvest rainwater. He was finally rescued by Brazilian fishermen.

The ashes of the creator of *Star Trek* have flown into space twice.

Gene Roddenberry created the first *Star Trek* television series. When he died in 1991, his body was cremated, and some of his ashes were flown into space and back to Earth onboard a 1992 Space Shuttle mission. Five years later, a Celestis rocket was launched, carrying his ashes back into space again.

FAST FACT!

The original *Star Trek* series ran for three seasons, and was extended into several other shows such as *Star Trek: Voyager* and *Deep Space Nine*.

A mysterious explosion in 1908 flattened more than 80 million trees.

The explosion occurred in Tunguska, a heavily forested part of Siberia, Russia. An area of about 830 square miles was devastated, and shock waves traveled right around Earth. To this day, scientists are not completely sure what caused the gigantic explosion.

Art students in London made a sculpture of King Kong entirely out of popcorn.

In 2003, students at the Camberwell College of Arts in London constructed a giant sculpture of the famous movie monster.

It took 630 hours to build the beast out of popcorn to celebrate the 70th anniversary of the first *King Kong* film. The finished sculpture stood 12.8 feet high and weighed more than 1,700 pounds— the weight of four real gorillas.

FAST FACT!

Currently, the largest ever popcorn sculpture is a 5-layer cake that stood just under 21 feet tall and weighed 11,685 pounds!

One Australian coin became more valuable melted down for its silver than for the coin's face value.

In 1966, a new Australian 50-cent piece was minted. The first coins were made of 80 percent silver and 20 percent copper, and were so large that three coins contained 1 ounce of silver.

As the price of silver soared in the world markets, the amount of silver in the coin was worth as much as four times the face value of the coin. They were withdrawn as currency soon afterward!

Danish pastries were originally from Austria, not Denmark, and Panama hats are from Ecuador, not Panama.

It's funny how some things get their names. The sweet pastries we call Danish were first baked in the Austrian city of Vienna. In the mid-nineteenth century, Austrian bakers working in Denmark first introduced the pastry, where it was developed further and became known as a Danish.

The Panama hat is made from the woven leaves of the toquilla straw plant. These plants and hats actually come from Ecuador, but became known as Panama hats because many Americans, including President Theodore Roosevelt, bought the hats in Panama.

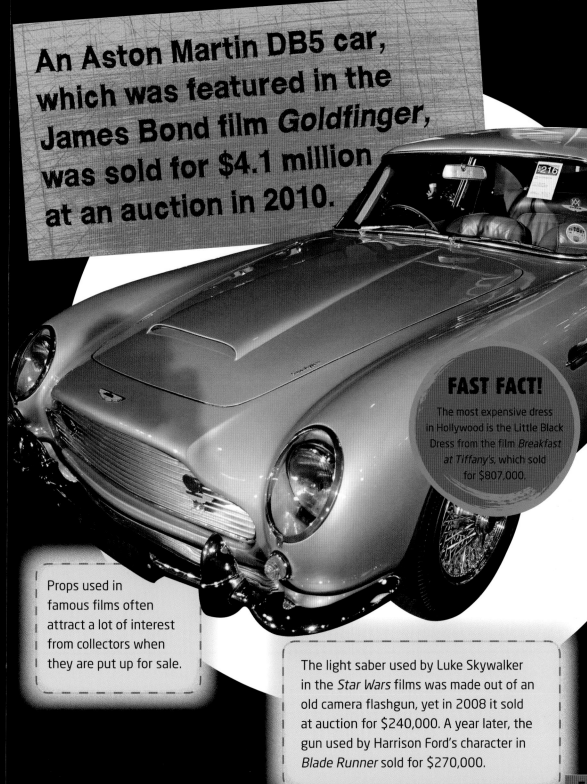

An Aston Martin DB5 car, which was featured in the James Bond film *Goldfinger*, was sold for $4.1 million at an auction in 2010.

FAST FACT!

The most expensive dress in Hollywood is the Little Black Dress from the film *Breakfast at Tiffany's*, which sold for $807,000.

Props used in famous films often attract a lot of interest from collectors when they are put up for sale.

The light saber used by Luke Skywalker in the *Star Wars* films was made out of an old camera flashgun, yet in 2008 it sold at auction for $240,000. A year later, the gun used by Harrison Ford's character in *Blade Runner* sold for $270,000.

A man survived a jet airliner flight across the Atlantic Ocean stowed away in the wheel housing of the plane.

In 1969, 17-year-old Armando Socarras Ramirez sought to escape from Cuba by stowing away inside the wheel housing of a DC-8 jet airliner bound for Spain.

FAST FACT!

Ramirez stuffed his ears with cotton balls to muffle the engine noise and wore shoes with rubber soles to help him climb up inside the wheel housing.

Ramirez endured icy cold temperatures of -40°F and he struggled to get enough oxygen due to the thin air, but he survived the journey and the touchdown at an airport in Madrid, Spain.

At just one drip per second, a faucet can leak 3,000 gallons per year.

If you care about not wasting water, get your parents to fix any dripping faucets in your house because the water they waste builds up quickly. Lots of water is wasted at home due to leaking hose connections too, but these drips are dwarfed by leaks in city water supply pipes.

According to *The New York Times*, the New York City water supply system loses 26 million gallons per year due to leaks.

An Alaska moose's antlers weigh more than a typical seven-year-old boy.

Alaska, or giant, moose live in Alaska and parts of northern Canada. They are the largest of all moose, standing more than 6.5 feet tall from hoof to shoulder, and reaching 8.8 feet in length.

FAST FACT!

Alaska moose have tough tongues. They have been known to use them to lick salt off the roads in icy weather.

A male moose's antlers can span more than 6 feet and weigh over 60 pounds. They are shed at the end of each year, and a new pair grows the following year.

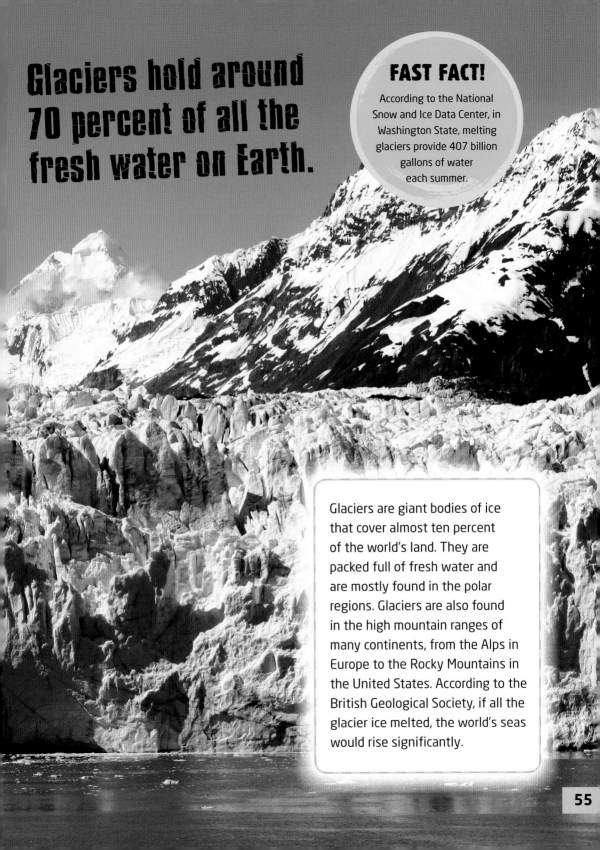

Glaciers hold around 70 percent of all the fresh water on Earth.

FAST FACT!

According to the National Snow and Ice Data Center, in Washington State, melting glaciers provide 407 billion gallons of water each summer.

Glaciers are giant bodies of ice that cover almost ten percent of the world's land. They are packed full of fresh water and are mostly found in the polar regions. Glaciers are also found in the high mountain ranges of many continents, from the Alps in Europe to the Rocky Mountains in the United States. According to the British Geological Society, if all the glacier ice melted, the world's seas would rise significantly.

Forces generated by a Formula One car would allow it to drive on a ceiling.

A Formula One (F1) car is one of the most advanced racing vehicles in the world. Its body generates a lot of downforce— a force that helps push the car's tires onto the track to improve grip.

At speeds of above 120 miles per hour, an F1 car generates more force than its own weight, which means that in theory, it could drive upside down without falling to the ground.

FAST FACT!

A Formula One car's engine and brakes are so powerful that the vehicle can go from zero to 100 miles per hour and back in just 5.5 seconds.

A South American bird barks instead of sings.

The Jocotoco Antpitta bird was discovered in 1997 in a remote part of the Andes mountain range of South America. Discovered by scientist Robert Ridgely, it is one of the largest new birds to be discovered in the past 50 years. The birds are about 8 to 9 inches in length, with long legs for hopping around on the rainforest floor.

The Jocotoco Antpitta bird's call is deeper than most other birds, and sounds more like a small dog's bark than birdsong.

FAST FACT!

A Jocotoco Antpitta eats worms, ants, and other insects. Its bark is worse than its bite; they are actually shy birds.

George Clooney used to sell insurance door-to-door, and Lady Gaga mopped floors.

FAST FACT!

One of Brad Pitt's first ever jobs was wearing a large chicken suit and dancing around to attract potential customers to a chicken restaurant in Los Angeles.

Before becoming a pop music sensation, Lady Gaga (then known as Stephani Germanotta), worked as a waitress, serving customers and mopping floors at a Greek restaurant in New York City.

Clooney tried out for professional baseball with the Cincinnati Reds, but when that didn't work out, he worked selling men's suits, insurance, and as a tobacco harvester before getting his big break in the TV series, *ER*.

A million American one-dollar bills weigh over 1,800 pounds.

The dollar bill is 6.14 inches long, 2.61 inches wide, and is 0.0043 inches thick. Over 40 percent of all bills printed in the United States are one dollar bills.

Each bill weighs just 0.03 ounces, so a million of them stacked together would weigh around 1,875 pounds and make a pile 358 feet high. As $100 bills are the same thickness and weight as single dollar bills, a million dollars in $100s would weigh 18.75 pounds.

FAST FACT!

The heaviest coin was produced by Canada. It consists of 99.99% gold, is 20 inches across, and weighs a total of 220 pounds.

Among the crazy weapons of World War II was a gun that could fire around corners and, planned but not used, bats fitted with bombs.

The *Krummlauf,* or "curved barrel" in English, was a bent barrel fitted to a German Sturmgewehr 44 assault rifle so soldiers could fire around corners in close combat.

The American forces, in contrast, tested out but didn't deploy, the idea of dropping thousands of Mexican free-tailed bats fitted with firebombs into Japanese towns, many of which were largely constructed of wooden buildings.

FAST FACT!

Other animals that were used during wartime include dolphins, rats, cats, and dogs.

One taxi driver in India only drives his taxi cab backward.

Harpeet Devi drove his taxi cab in Punjab, India, in a regular way until his car gearbox got stuck and would only work in reverse. While saving up to have the gearbox fixed, Devi drove the cab backward. He got to like it so much that he actually had his car converted to drive backward, with four reverse gears and a special siren to warn other motorists!

FAST FACT!

In 1907, New York businessman Harry N. Allen was the first to paint his taxis yellow because this color made the vehicles more visible.

India Limited
Cares For KolKatta

If Earth's history were shrunk into 24 hours then humans first appeared less than two minutes before the end of the last hour.

11 12 1 2

Earth was formed approximately 4.54 billion years ago, but homo sapiens—human beings as we know them—were pretty late arrivals. Scientists estimate that humans started developing 150,000 to 200,000 years ago. So if Earth's history started at 0:00 and ran for 24 hours, then humans arrived later than 11:58 p.m.—two minutes to midnight.

Robert Baden-Powell, founder of the scouting movement, was a successful British spy.

Robert Baden-Powell founded the scouting movement for boys and girls, and wrote *Scouting for Boys* in 1908—a book that sold over 150 million copies.

FAST FACT!

Today, there are nearly 32 million scouts all over the world. Two-thirds of the world's scouts live in developing countries.

In the nineteenth century, however, Baden-Powell was in the British Army and often worked as a spy, gathering information on enemy positions. He would sometimes pretend to be a slightly eccentric naturalist, drawing flowers, butterflies, and other insects in a large sketchbook. These illustrations were actually coded pictures showing the positions of fortifications and gun emplacements.

The Australian town of Coober Pedy has homes, hotels, and even a church underground.

Coober Pedy is a small Australian mining town famous for producing most of the world's opal gemstones. About half of its 3,000 residents live underground in homes burrowed out of the rock, because life beneath the surface is cooler than the desert heat above. There is also an underground church—St. Peter and Paul's Catholic Church—and even an underground campsite where visitors can pitch their tents.

FAST FACT!

Coober Pedy's golf course is made up of sand, not grass.

Batman's car in the original TV series was made from a concept car that was bought for only one dollar.

In 1955, a futuristic one-off car was hand-built in Italy for the Lincoln car company at a cost of about $250,000. Called the Lincoln Futura, it was displayed at auto shows and then retired.

A decade later, car customizer George Barris bought the vehicle for one dollar and, with the aid of metalworkers and designers, produced the Batmobile– a sleek, 18.7-foot-long vehicle with giant tail fins.

Taisto Miettinen was World Wife-Carrying Champion in 2009, 2010, and 2011.

The World Wife-Carrying Championships began in the small town of Sonkajärvi in Finland in the mid-1990s. The competition involves racing around a course, often including obstacles such as water jumps, with men carrying their wives or partners over their shoulders.

Taisto Miettinen is a Finnish lawyer who has become three-time world champion. The 2011 event was watched by a crowd of over 6,000 spectators and featured 43 racers from 10 different countries.

FAST FACT!

The Wife-Carrying world record is 55.5 seconds, set by an Estonian couple in 2001.

One Middle Eastern skyscraper is so tall it takes 3 months just to clean its windows.

FAST FACT!

The Eiffel Tower in Paris, France, was the tallest building in the world at the time of its completion in 1889 and remained so for over 40 years.

When the 2,716 foot tall Burj Khalifa skyscraper was completed in 2010, it was declared the tallest inhabited building in the world. It contains hundreds of apartments linked by 57 elevators and 8 escalators and has more than 24,000 windows. It takes 90 days for a team of 36 human workers and automatic machines to clean them all.

Built between 1962 and 1965, the Peel P50 was tiny, measuring 4 feet 5 inches long, 3 feet 3 inches wide, and 3 feet 5 inches high. It weighed a mere 131 pounds—less than most adult drivers—and was powered by a puny 49cc moped engine, giving the car a top speed of less than 40 mph. Parking, though, was easy. Drivers just got out of the car and pulled it into position by hand!

The world's smallest production car, the Peel P50, weighed less than its driver.

FAST FACT!

In 2010, a new replica of the Peel P50 was built. It was powered by a tiny electric motor, which gave the vehicle a top speed of just 10 mph.

FMP 62B

Homer, Marge, Lisa, and Maggie are the real-life first names of *The Simpsons'* creator Matt Groening's father, mother, and two sisters.

Matt Groening's funny cartoon family first appeared on television in 1987 as short excerpts in the *Tracy Ullman Show*. Two years later, it became a full-length show in its own right and proved an instant hit. Over 500 episodes have been made, winning 27 Emmy awards. It has now become the longest continually running sitcom on American TV.

It's free to mail letters inside Andorra.

Andorra is an independent country located along the border between France and Spain. Its population of just under 60,000 mostly work in tourism, because the country has many thriving winter sports resorts.

But Andorra has no postal service of its own. Instead, France and Spain operate the country's mail system. Any letters you wish to mail inside Andorra are free to send!

Ancient Egyptian pharaoh Tutankhamen was buried with 32 pairs of sandals and 139 walking sticks.

When an expedition led by Howard Carter unearthed Tutankhamen's tomb in the 1920s, they got quite a surprise! Apart from the magnificent funeral coffin housing his body, Tutankhamen's tomb was packed with thousands of objects including ostrich feather fans, a bronze trumpet, a gold dagger, 30 jars of wine, and six full-sized chariots.

FAST FACT!

Tutankhamen became pharaoh when he was only nine years old. A total of over 3,000 treasures were placed in his tomb for his afterlife.

A British aristocrat used to throw expensive dinner parties just for his dogs.

Francis Egerton was born in 1756 and became the 8th Earl of Bridgewater in 1823. He sat at the dinner table with his dogs because he preferred dogs to people. Each dog was dressed in fashionable clothes and was attended by its own human servant.

Egerton wore a pair of shoes only once, leaving them in rows so that he could tell how many days had passed.

One of the first-ever computers weighed 29 tons. All its functions can now be shrunk onto a single microchip.

FAST FACT!

HP, Google, Microsoft, and Apple are all very successful IT companies, but they were all started in people's garages.

The computer in question was the Electronic Numerical Integrator and Computer (or ENIAC, for short) completed in 1946 at the University of Pennsylvania's Moore School of Engineering. This beast of a machine consisted of banks of circuits and measured 80 feet long, 8 feet high, and about 3.5 feet deep.

In 1996, computer scientists at the University of Pennsylvania built their own version of ENIAC on a silicon microchip the size of your fingernail.

President William Taft was so tone deaf that he had to be nudged when the American national anthem was played so that he could stand up.

Taft, the 27th President of the United States from 1909 to 1915, holds a number of notable firsts. These include being the first President to own a car and the first person to be the head of two branches of the American government, when he became Chief Justice of the Supreme Court in 1921. He was also the last President to keep a cow (his was called Pauline) on the White House lawn.

FAST FACT!

President Taft was so large (he weighed over 330 pounds) he needed a new, bigger bath after he got stuck in the first one.

An Olympic rower lost his gold medal in the lake on which he won the competition.

In 1956, Soviet Union rower Vyacheslav Ivanov won the single sculls race at the Melbourne Olympics in Australia. The 18 year old was delighted, then dismayed, as he accidentally dropped his gold medal into Lake Wendouree after the medal ceremony.

FAST FACT!

Ivanov was the first man to win the Olympic single sculls race three times in a row— 1956, 1960, and 1964.

The authorities took pity on Ivanov, and later presented him with a substitute gold medal.

In 2006, a man bought an original copy of the Declaration of Independence from a thrift store for just $2.48.

Michael Sparks, a musical equipment technician, bought several items from a thrift store in Nashville—salt and pepper shakers, a candleholder, and what he thought was a modern reprint of the Declaration of Independence.

His "reprint" turned out to be one of the 200 copies (of which only around 30 survive) of the official document printed in 1823. The following year, Sparks put it up for auction where it was sold for $477,650. Quite a profit!

Crickets hear through their knees.

Crickets are insects known for the chirping sound the males make by rubbing their wings together. There are over 900 different species of cricket. What is less well known is that crickets have a form of eardrum or, to give it its scientific term, tympanic membrane, located just below the middle joint of each front leg. These act as ears, allowing a cricket to hear other crickets.

FAST FACT!

Male crickets have a courting song to attract and impress nearby females.

American Ashrita Furman holds over 120 world records, including the longest distance traveled on a pogo stick.

Ashrita Furman just cannot help himself. The health food shop manager from New York broke his first world record in 1979 and has broken 399 records since.

FAST FACT!

Want more of Furman's feats? In 2007, he performed the most forward rolls in an hour (1,330) and in 2010 he built the largest see-saw at over 79 feet long.

His achievements include creating the largest lollipop (6,514 pounds) in 2008 and, in 2011, eating the most mashed potatoes in a minute (1 pound 7.9 ounces).

In 2010, retail chain Walmart's revenues were greater than the entire economy of Norway.

WAL★MART

Walmart employs over 2 million people around the world. The company's revenue in 2010 was a whooping $421.89 billion. One measure of a country's economy is gross domestic product, or GDP for short.

The GDP is the value of all the goods and services produced in a country in a year. Norway's GDP for 2010 was estimated by the World Bank as $417.46 billion.

Lyndon B. Johnson, Sting, Stephen King, J.K. Rowling, and Billy Crystal all worked as schoolteachers before they were famous.

Singer Sting used to teach at a convent school in England, while Stephen King wrote his famous novel, *Salem's Lot*, at night while working as a teacher at Hampden Academy in Maine.

FAST FACT!

Other odd jobs famous people have had include lion tamer (actor Christopher Walken) and clown (actor Hugh Jackman).

Long before he became President, Lyndon B. Johnson was a principal at the Welhausen School in Cotulla, Texas, and later taught public speaking at both Pearsall High School and Sam Houston High. Billy Crystal was a junior high school teacher on Long Island, while J.K. Rowling taught English in Portugal.

The can opener was invented decades after the tin can!

FAST FACT!

One of the earliest can openers from 1865 featured a bull's head design.

Storing food in metal cans began in the Netherlands in the eighteenth century. The first large canning factories sprang up in Britain, France, and the United States between 1813 and 1822, but can openers didn't arrive until the 1850s. The first can opener with a wheel to grip the edge of the can arrived even later in 1870.

Before can openers existed, people used whatever tools they could to puncture, chisel, or cut through the metal can.

One queen was so scared of fleas she had a tiny cannon built to fire cannonballs at them.

Queen Christina was a Swedish monarch who was born in 1626 and died in 1689. She is said to have ordered the construction of the mini silver cannon (10 inches long) to fire tiny cannonballs at fleas in her bedroom.

She wasn't the only one with a dislike of small creatures. English historian and politician Sir George Sitwell invented a tiny revolver so that he could shoot wasps in his garden.

J is the only letter that doesn't appear on the periodic table of elements.

The periodic table used in science classes is based on a table developed by the Russian scientist Dmitri Ivanovich Mendeleev from 1869 onward.

Each chemical element has a one-, two-, or three-letter chemical symbol. Apart from J, every letter of the alphabet is featured—from A (Al, Aluminum and Au, Gold) to Z (Zn, Zinc and Zr, Zirconium).

The volcanic eruption of Krakatoa in 1883 was heard 3,000 miles away in Alice Springs, Australia.

Lying between the Indonesian islands of Java and Sumatra, Krakatoa's volcano erupted with enormous force. Dust and stones were sent as high as 34 miles up into the atmosphere, the island was ripped apart by the force, and giant 100-feet-high tsunami waves battered coastlines. The sound was heard across a large part of the world. People on Rodriguez Island in the Indian Ocean reported a sound like heavy gunfire, even though they were over 2,900 miles away.

FAST FACT!

Fine ashes from the Krakatoa explosion made it all the way to New York City!

The famous Dr. Seuss book, *Green Eggs and Ham*, was written on a bet.

In the late 1950s, Theodor Seuss Geisel had just written his famous Dr. Seuss book, *The Cat In The Hat*, using just 236 different words to help children learn to read. Then his publisher, Bennett Alfred Cerf, bet him that he couldn't write a successful children's book using even fewer words.

FAST FACT!

Dr Seuss was not a real doctor —he just added the title to his name for fun. His first book was rejected by 27 publishers.

Geisel returned with *Green Eggs and Ham*, featuring only 50 different words. Both of these Dr. Seuss books have sold over 7 million copies in the United States alone.

Google's first computer was fitted into a case made of LEGO bricks.

In 1996, Stanford University students Larry Page and Sergey Brin were building a computer to test their search engine program, called Pagerank, which became the core of the Google search engine.

FAST FACT!

In 2011, the Google company earned over $37 billion—more than enough to buy the LEGO group company many times over.

Having bought ten expensive hard disks to store all their data, Page and Brin needed a cheap case for their computer, so they built it out of LEGO bricks and plastic sheeting.

The first-known printed use of the word "nerd" was in a Dr. Seuss children's book.

A nerd is now a nickname for someone who is clever, often wears glasses, uses computers, or studies hard and reads books intensely. But when it first appeared in Dr. Seuss' 1950 children's book, *If I Ran the Zoo*, it was the name of an imaginary creature. From the 1960s onward, the word became a popular way to describe a bookish person.

FAST FACT!

Dr. Seuss' birthday, March 2nd, is now commemorated as National Read Across America Day.

In 1991, there was just one World Wide Web website. Today, there are more than 230 million.

The World Wide Web is used by hundreds of millions of people every day to learn, swap information, buy and sell goods, and for entertainment. So, it's hard to get your head around how relatively new an invention it really is. British computer expert, Tim Berners-Lee, working at the CERN Institute in Switzerland developed the first website, which went online at http://info.cern.ch in the summer of 1991.

FAST FACT!

Google estimated the Internet at about 5 million terabytes of data, which is 5 billion gigabytes or 5 trillion megabytes.

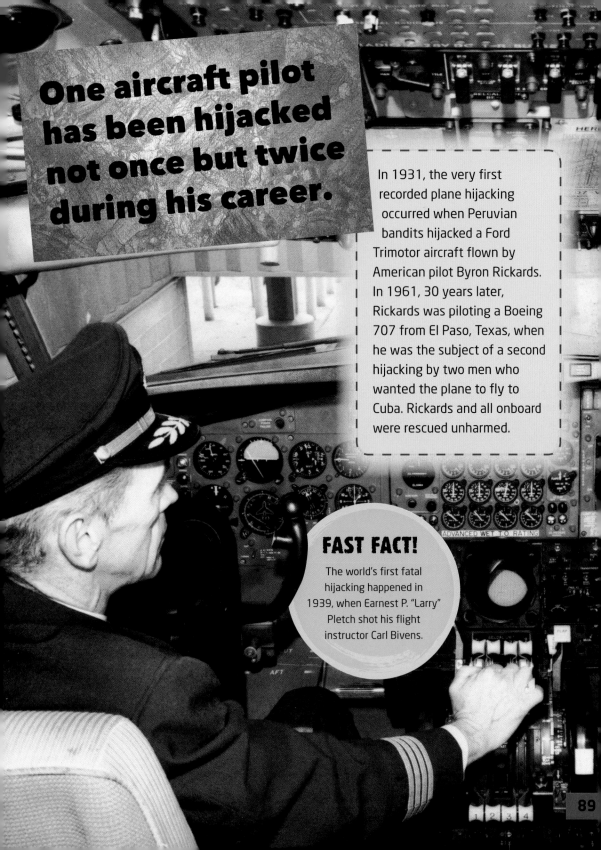

One aircraft pilot has been hijacked not once but twice during his career.

In 1931, the very first recorded plane hijacking occurred when Peruvian bandits hijacked a Ford Trimotor aircraft flown by American pilot Byron Rickards. In 1961, 30 years later, Rickards was piloting a Boeing 707 from El Paso, Texas, when he was the subject of a second hijacking by two men who wanted the plane to fly to Cuba. Rickards and all onboard were rescued unharmed.

FAST FACT!

The world's first fatal hijacking happened in 1939, when Earnest P. "Larry" Pletch shot his flight instructor Carl Bivens.

A newborn kangaroo is small enough to fit in a teaspoon.

Kangaroos give birth to really tiny babies that can weigh less than a tenth of an ounce. The newly born kangaroo lives in a special pouch called a marsupium on the mother's body for several months until large enough to enter the world on its own.

The largest species of kangaroo—the red kangaroo—can grow taller than an adult human and weigh more than 200 pounds.

FAST FACT!

A red kangaroo can jump spectacularly far. An adult male red kangaroo can cover up to 25 feet in a single leap.

Grand Theft Auto IV was the most expensive computer game on its release, costing $100 million to make.

Created by Rockstar Games, this action-adventure game cost more to make than many Hollywood films. It took over 1,000 people three-and-a-half years to produce the game, which includes many hours of music tracks and complex action scenes. Within three years of its 2008 release, the game sold more than 22 million copies.

grand theft auto IV

The Bombardier 415 fire-fighting aircraft can scoop up to 1,620 gallons of water in just 12 seconds.

Firefighters tackling large forest and bush fires use water bombing aircraft that can skim a lake or the sea to scoop up large quantities of water. The aircraft then fly over the blaze and dump their load on the fire. The *Bombardier 415 Superscooper* has a wingspan of almost 94 feet and can take off and land from water or the ground. More than 70 of these aircraft have been built. They operate in the United States, Canada, France, Italy, and Croatia.

A nuclear power engineer working for NASA invented the Super Soaker toy water gun.

After a spell working at the Air Force Weapons Laboratory in the 1970s, Alabama-born Lonnie G. Johnson moved to California to work at NASA's Jet Propulsion Laboratory. There he helped to develop the nuclear power plant that was fitted to the *Galileo* space probe traveling to Jupiter. In 1989, when he was tinkering at home on designs for more powerful and fun water guns, he invented the first Super Soaker—now a best-selling brand of water guns that have sold millions.

FAST FACT!

The Super Soaker is just one of Johnson's 62 patents, ranging from hair-drying rollers to a wet-diaper detector.

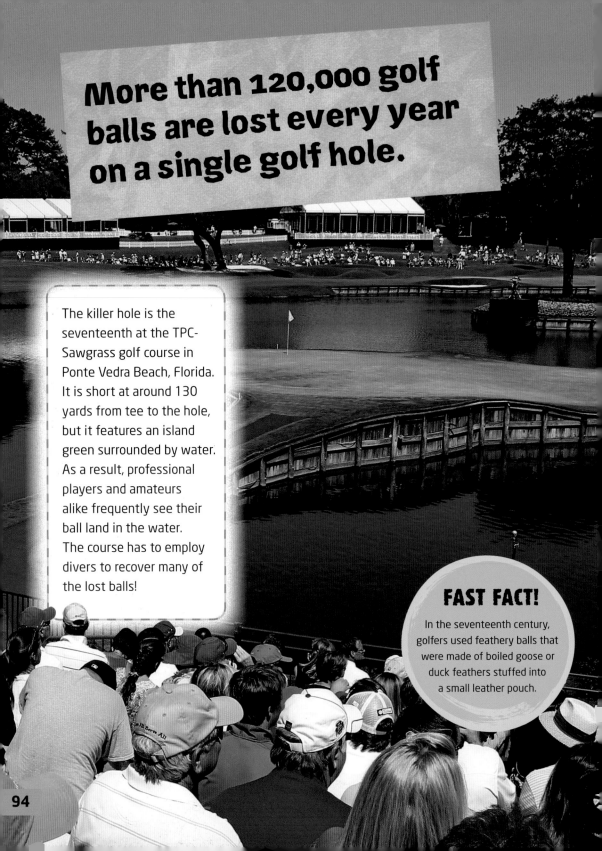

More than 120,000 golf balls are lost every year on a single golf hole.

The killer hole is the seventeenth at the TPC-Sawgrass golf course in Ponte Vedra Beach, Florida. It is short at around 130 yards from tee to the hole, but it features an island green surrounded by water. As a result, professional players and amateurs alike frequently see their ball land in the water. The course has to employ divers to recover many of the lost balls!

FAST FACT!

In the seventeenth century, golfers used feathery balls that were made of boiled goose or duck feathers stuffed into a small leather pouch.

The dwarf planet Pluto was named by an 11-year-old schoolgirl.

Some people think that the planet was named after the Disney animated dog, but it's actually the other way around. The planet got its name in 1930 when schoolgirl Venetia Burney from Oxford, UK, suggested the name *Pluto*, the Roman god of the underworld, to her grandfather when they were discussing the newly discovered planet. He contacted his friend, astronomer Herbert Hall Turner. In less than two months, *Pluto* became the official name of the planet.

An inventor made more than 5,000 different prototypes of his invention before getting it right.

FAST FACT!

Hubert Cecil Booth invented one of the first motorized vacuum cleaners. It was enormous, and had to be moved by horses.

British engineer Sir James Dyson hit upon a novel way of producing a more efficient vacuum cleaner, using swirling cyclones of air to suck up dirt and dust without the need for a messy bag.

He had to make a staggering 5,127 prototypes of the machine before his DC01 vacuum cleaner went on sale in the early 1990s. But Dyson now has a fortune of about $1.5 billion as a result of his hard work.

An NBA basketball player once scored 100 points in a single game.

That player was the great Wilt "The Stilt" Chamberlain and he managed the feat playing for the Philadelphia Warriors against the New York Knicks in 1962. The 7 foot 1 inch scoring machine notched 23 points in the first quarter, 18 in the second, 28 in the third, and 31 points in the fourth, totaling 100 points in the 48-minute game. What makes it even more amazing is that it was in an era before players could score three points for a long-range basket—all of Wilt's points came from two-point shots or one point free throws.

FAST FACT!

In the 1961/62 season, Wilt Chamberlain scored an average of 50.4 points in each of the 80 games he played. Today, this record is thought to be unbreakable.

The tallest dam in the world stands three times higher than the Statue of Liberty.

Dams are built to hold water for farming, to create a town water supply, or to generate electricity at a hydro-electric power station. The oldest-known dam is in Jordan, and is about 5,000 years old. The world's tallest dam—the Nurek Dam in the central Asian nation of Tajikistan—is much younger. It was completed in 1980 after 19 years of work, and measures 2,300 feet in length and 984 feet in height.

A monster truck once jumped over a Boeing 727 airliner.

Monster trucks are souped-up pick-up trucks with giant wheels and massive suspension systems, and they thrill fans by racing around obstacle courses or making spectacular jumps. In 1999, Dan Runte and his vehicle—the Bigfoot 14 monster truck—reached a speed of 69 mph, leaping over a Boeing 727 airliner, recording a jump of 202 feet. That's one of the longest jumps ever made by a monster truck.

More rain fell in a day in Mumbai, India, than Chicago typically receives in a year.

You think of a heavy rain day when one inch of rain falls on your home town. The city of Chicago, for example, averages about 34 inches of rainfall in an entire year. But on July 26, 2005, a staggering 39.1 inches of rain fell in 24 hours in Mumbai. The resulting floods were devastating. The city's airports were shut down, thousands of trucks, buses, and taxis were damaged or destroyed, and at least 5,000 people died.

FAST FACT!

In contrast to the monsoon rains of Mumbai, parts of Chile are really, really dry. The average rainfall in the Antofagasta region is just 0.04 inch per year.

When you think of robots, you might think of space probes crawling around the surface of Mars, or robotic arms spray painting and welding cars in factories. But the most common robot on the planet is a small, disc-shaped, wheeled machine that navigates its own way around the house, vacuum cleaning the floors.

There are more robotic vacuum cleaners than any other type of robot in the world.

FAST FACT!

Roombas are so clever that they can sense the dirty areas in a room and spend a longer time cleaning them.

The first Roomba cleaning bot, built by iRobot, was launched in 2002. Since that time, more than 5 million Roombas have been sold, making it the world's most popular robot.

Bubblewrap was originally invented as wallpaper.

In 1957, Alfred W. Fielding and Marc Chavannes sealed two plastic shower curtains together, capturing air bubbles between them. Bubblewrap was born. The pair thought it would make funky wallpaper, but when it didn't sell well they offered it as insulation to keep heat inside greenhouses.

FAST FACT!

One extreme test—to show the power of bubblewrap —included wrapping up a pumpkin and dropping it from 35 feet. It survived without a scratch!

It was only when computer companies started to use bubblewrap to protect their hardware that sales of the material boomed. Now, enough bubblewrap is produced each year to circle Earth more than ten times.

An astronaut lost a $100,000 toolbag in space.

NASA astronaut Heidemarie Stefanyshyn-Piper was a veteran of over 30 hours of spacewalks. But in 2009, while out in space repairing part of a solar panel powering the International Space Station, she had a major mishap.

A grease gun inside her toolbag had pumped grease all over the bag. As she tried to clean it up, the bag containing expensive tools floated away and out of reach. The toolbag orbited Earth for nine months before burning up in the planet's atmosphere.

A lion's roar can be heard up to 5 miles away.

These kings and queens of the African plains are one of only a handful of cats, including jaguars and leopards, which can produce a loud, deep roar—partly due to a special jointed bone in their throat called a hyoid. Of all the big cats, lions roar the most and the loudest.

An average male lion is 9 feet long, weighs around 350 to 450 pounds, and is very lazy. The males let the lionesses do more than three quarters of the hunting, and rest for up to 20 hours a day.

The winner of the Olympic women's 100-meter sprint turned out to be a man.

Stanislawa Walasiewiczowna (known as Stella Walsh) was born in Poland in 1911. She competed for Poland at the 1932 Olympics held in Los Angeles, and won a gold medal in the 100-meter sprint. Four years later she won a second medal—a silver—at the Berlin Olympics. After her death in 1980, though, an autopsy revealed that Stella was in fact a man.

FAST FACT!

Stella Walsh's 18 world records and two Olympic medals were not stripped from the record books after her death.

During World War II, the U.S. military tried to develop pigeon-guided missiles.

American scientist B.F. Skinner received funding during World War II to build a missile control system. Pigeons were trained to tap on a screen showing the target while inside the missile.

FAST FACT!

Cher Ami was a World War I carrier pigeon that helped to save the lives of 200 trapped American troops by carrying a message about their location.

The missiles were never made, but pigeons were used in both World War I and II to ferry important messages. They were also used as experimental aerial photographers, carrying tiny automatic cameras to take pictures of the battlefields below.

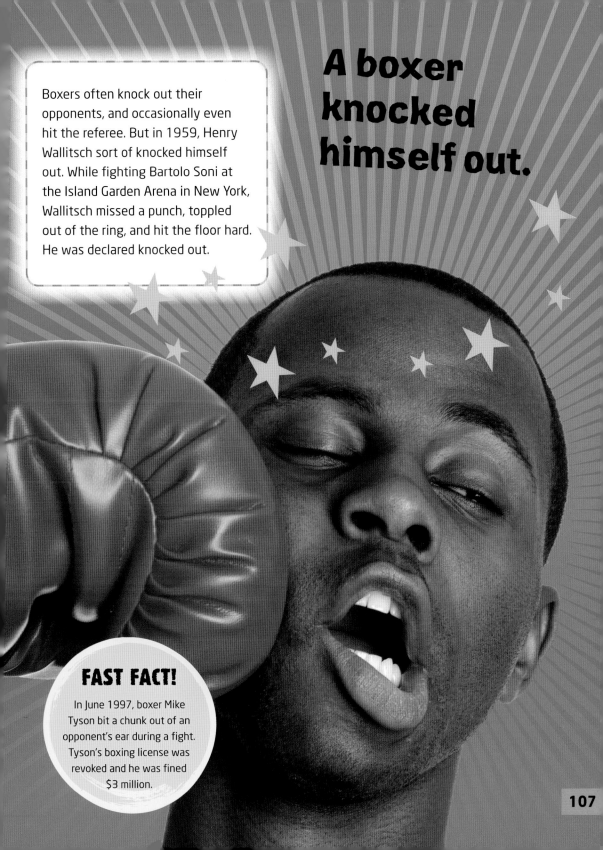

Boxers often knock out their opponents, and occasionally even hit the referee. But in 1959, Henry Wallitsch sort of knocked himself out. While fighting Bartolo Soni at the Island Garden Arena in New York, Wallitsch missed a punch, toppled out of the ring, and hit the floor hard. He was declared knocked out.

A boxer knocked himself out.

FAST FACT!

In June 1997, boxer Mike Tyson bit a chunk out of an opponent's ear during a fight. Tyson's boxing license was revoked and he was fined $3 million.

PHOTO CREDITS